D1519149

RANDY ORTON:
THE VIPER

Fly!

An Imprint of Abdo Zoom

abdobooks.com

KENNY ABDO

abdobooks.com

Published by Abdo Zoom, a division of ABDO, P.O. Box 398166, Minneapolis, Minnesota 55439. Copyright © 2020 by Abdo Consulting Group, Inc. International copyrights reserved in all countries. No part of this book may be reproduced in any form without written permission from the publisher. Fly!™ is a trademark and logo of Abdo Zoom.

Printed in the United States of America, North Mankato, Minnesota.
052019
092019

Photo Credits: Alamy, AP images, Getty Images, Icon Sportswire, Seth Poppel/Yearbook Library, Shutterstock, © Shamsuddin Muhammad p.cover, p1 / CC BY 2.0, © Ed Webster p4, p14 / CC BY 2.0, © Megan Elice Meadows p5, p14 / CC BY-SA 2.0, © Miguel Discart p11, p16, / CC BY-SA 2.0, © Tabercil p16 / CC BY-SA 3.0
Production Contributors: Kenny Abdo, Jennie Forsberg, Grace Hansen
Design Contributors: Dorothy Toth, Neil Klinepier

Library of Congress Control Number: 2018963795

Publisher's Cataloging-in-Publication Data

Names: Abdo, Kenny, author.
Title: Randy Orton: the viper / by Kenny Abdo.
Other title: The viper
Description: Minneapolis, Minnesota : Abdo Zoom, 2020 | Series: Wrestling biographies set 2 | Includes online resources and index.
Identifiers: ISBN 9781532127533 (lib. bdg.) | ISBN 9781532128516 (ebook) | ISBN 9781532129001 (Read-to-me ebook)
Subjects: LCSH: Orton, Randy (Randal Orton)--Juvenile literature. | Wrestlers--United States--Biography--Juvenile literature. | World Wrestling Entertainment Studios--Juvenile literature.
Classification: DDC 796.812092 [B]--dc23

TABLE OF
CONTENTS

RANDY ORTON

Randy Orton, aka "The Viper," is one of the most recognizable names in the WWE!

Winning many **championship titles**, Orton has been dominating the **ring** and taking down legends for nearly two decades!

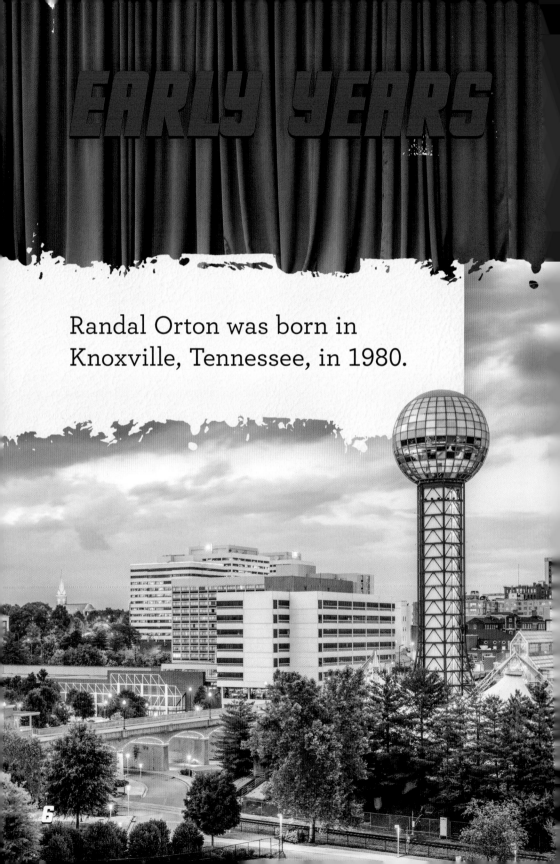

Randal Orton was born in
Knoxville, Tennessee, in 1980.

He went to high school in Missouri, where he wrestled as an **amateur**. After graduating, Orton joined the United States Marines. He was **discharged** for bad conduct shortly after.

Orton is a third-generation
professional wrestler. His dad is
famous wrestler "Cowboy" Bob Orton.
His uncle Barry Orton and grandfather
Bob Orton Senior were also fighters.
Cowboy Bob helped train Randy.

Orton made his WWE television **debut** on SmackDown. on April 25, 2002. He fought and defeated Hardcore Holly.

Orton gave himself the nickname "The Legend Killer" in 2004. He would disrespect and then battle admired fighters of the past.

Throughout the years, Orton
retired legends like Hulk Hogan,
The Undertaker, and Mick Foley!

During SmackDown Live in 2016, the Wyatt Family helped Orton defeat Kane in a match. They all teamed up and together won the SmackDown **Tag Team Championship**. Orton went on to win the **Royal Rumble** match in 2017.

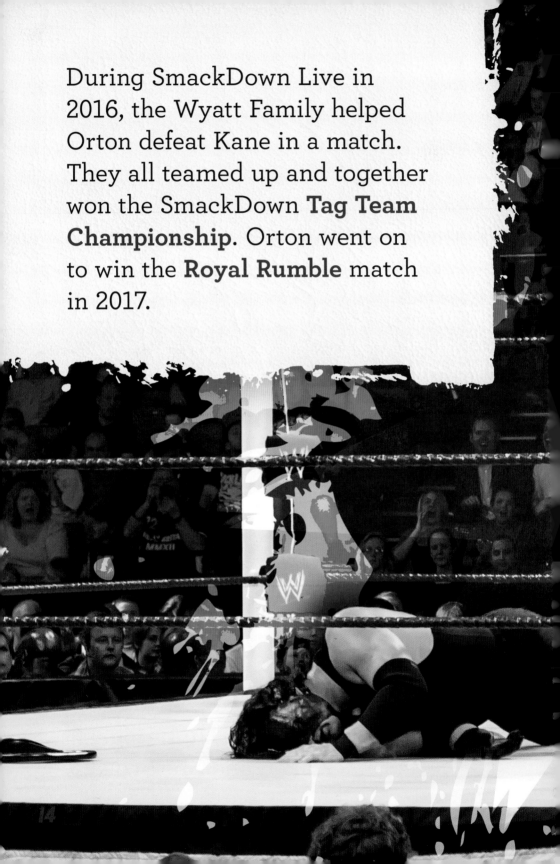

Orton fought Bobby Roode for the United States **Championship** at Fastlane in 2018. Orton won the **title**. He had become the 18th Grand Slam Champion of WWE.

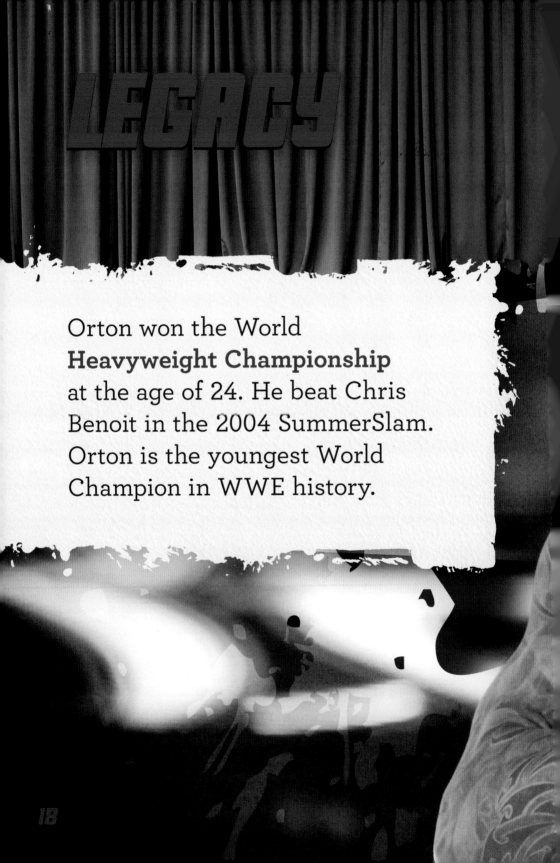

LEGACY

Orton won the World **Heavyweight Championship** at the age of 24. He beat Chris Benoit in the 2004 SummerSlam. Orton is the youngest World Champion in WWE history.

He has starred in many movies and TV shows. Orton appeared in the movie *Changeland*, co-starring Seth Green and Macaulay Culkin, in 2019.

RANDY ORTON

12 ROUNDS 2
RELOADED

GLOSSARY

amateur – an athlete who fights non-professionally without pay.

championship – a game, match, or race held to find a first-place winner.

debut – to appear for the first time.

discharge – to be asked to leave service for bad behavior.

heavyweight – a division for larger athletes.

ring – the stage where wrestling matches take place.

Royal Rumble – a major WWE show held every year in January.

tag team – a division made up of teams of two people. Wrestlers tag their partner to get in and out of the match.

title – the position of being the best in that division.

ONLINE RESOURCES

Booklinks
NONFICTION NETWORK
FREE! ONLINE NONFICTION RESOURCES

To learn more about Randy Orton, please visit **abdobooklinks.com** or scan this QR code. These links are routinely monitored and updated to provide the most current information available.

INDEX